THE KIDS' BOOK OF

FRIENDS

How to make friends
and be a friend

To my family: Raúl, Oto, and my mum and dad, Jen and Dan, for their support and patience!
To the friends of my heart, old and new.
And to Hiruni, for illustrating friendship so beautifully.

Copyright @WoodenHouseBooks, 2022.
Catherine Stephenson

Illustrated by Hiruni Kariyawasam

First Printing, 2022
ISBN 9798363261220
Wooden House Books
www.woodenhousebooks.com

FRIENDS can be awesome!

There are lots of people in the world, but only a few special ones will become your friends. Whether you're 5, 9 or 95, it can be great to have a friend!

So what does a friend look like? How do you make friends? What do friends do that is special? What happens if the friendship changes?

TO FIND OUT, FOLLOW TWINS FRIDA AND FREDDIE.

FRIENDS can be surprisingly similar to you...
or surprisingly different.

You're short, they're tall. You're quiet, they talk non-stop. You like drawing, they like basketball. You never know what your friends will look like or what interests they will have.

FRIENDS can appear in unexpected places.

You might make a friend in the park, at the bus stop, or while paddling on a river! They could be a relative, a teacher, a neighbor, or even an animal. Miaow!

To make new FRIENDS, try saying hi.

Smile, and ask someone what their name is, or if they want to play.

FRIENDS can listen. FRIENDS can help.

Listening shows you care. And if your friend feels sad or worried, you can cheer them up or help them.

FRIENDS can be loyal.

Encourage your friend, support them, cheer them on! And stand up for them if someone else is unkind to them (or to anyone else — being mean isn't cool).

FRIENDS can share.

It's fun to share toys, games and good times. Friends can also share thoughts, feelings, and ideas.

FRIENDS can be themselves with each other.

Remember, it's ok to still be you! Friends should make you feel safe and able to be yourself. If a friend makes you feel uncomfortable, you can talk to a trusted adult.

FRIENDS can argue sometimes.

You might need to have a break from each other. Try and talk about it if you can...everyone sees things differently, and talking is the way to understand others' views.

It's ok to not get it right... FRIENDS can make mistakes.

If your friend hurts you, try telling them. And if you make a mistake, apologize — nobody gets things right all the time!

FRIENDS don't need to be together all the time.

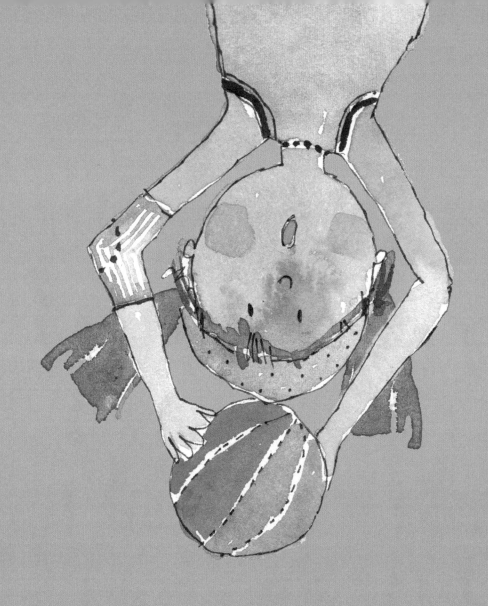

It's ok to do your own thing, and spend time on your own, or with other people. Having different types of friends makes life more interesting!

FRIENDS sometimes move on, and that's ok.

Just like you're growing and changing all the time, friendships can change. Friends might drift apart, or one of you might move to a new place. Sometimes you might feel you have more friends, sometimes less.

FRIENDS are kind.

Friends try to be kind, in what they do and say.
Remember also to be kind and a friend to yourself. Sometimes
children can worry about friendships — talking to someone in
your family or a teacher can help.

Wait, is that Freddie? Where's he going?!

PEOPLE need PEOPLE.

If you see someone who looks lonely or unhappy, maybe talk to them, or see if they want to join in your game. A new friend is a new world to discover — what are you waiting for?

FRIDA AND FREDDIE'S STORY OF FRIENDS ENDS HERE FOR TODAY. ENJOY YOUR OWN JOURNEY OF FRIENDSHIP. IT WILL LAST YOUR WHOLE LIFE... AND IT WILL BE SPECIAL AND UNIQUE, JUST LIKE YOU!

A MESSAGE FROM THE AUTHOR

Dear Reader,

A HUGE thank you for choosing "The Kids' Book of Friends" from the many on the shelf. I hope you and your family enjoyed it!

This is my debut book, so any feedback you have would be extremely helpful. If you could spare a few minutes to leave me a review on Amazon (or wherever you hang out outline), I'll read it with great interest. As you probably know, reviews are super important for writers!

Thank you again for your support, and can't wait to hear from you.

Catherine

Don't miss our new releases and special offers and sign up to Wooden House Books Club. Scan the QR or go to:
http://woodenhousebooks.com/dont-miss-the-latest-news

ABOUT CATHERINE

Catherine was born in the UK, and as a child, read many magical books. When she grew up, she traveled to work in Spain to teach English for a year. She now lives with her partner, son and two cats in Barcelona. She is a freelance writer and translator from Spanish and Catalan into English. 'The Kids' Book of Friends' is her debut children's book. Away from work, you'll find her in the mountains with a camera round her neck, or with her nose in a book in front of the fire.

ABOUT HIRUNI

Hiruni is from Sri Lanka, where she lives with her family in a town called Ambalangoda. She holds a Bachelor's Degree in Fashion Design from Moratuwa, one of Sri Lanka's leading universities. She enjoys doing paintings, fine illustrations, and illustrations for children's books in her unique style, mixing digital and watercolour techniques. In her free time, she's also an avid reader.

You can find us at:

WOODEN HOUSE BOOKS

woodenhousebooks.com
IG @woodenhousebooks

Made in the USA
Middletown, DE
29 November 2022

16470022R00018